Hatshepsut

Egypt's Woman King

by
Lorraine Jean Hopping

CELEBRATION PRESS
Pearson Learning Group

The following people from **Pearson Learning Group**
have contributed to the development of this product:

Leslie Feierstone Barna, Cindy Kane **Editorial**
Dorothea Fox, Joan Mazzeo **Design**
Salita Mehta **Photo Research**
Dan Trush **Art Buying**
Content Area Consultant Dr. Daniel J. Gelo

Marketing Christine Fleming
Publishing Operations Jennifer Van Der Heide
Production/Manufacturing Laura Benford-Sullivan,
Susan Levine, Michele Uhl

The following people from **DK** have
contributed to the development of this program:

Art Director Rachael Foster
Scarlett O'Hara **Managing Editor** | **Editor UK Editions** Marie Greenwood

Photo Credits: All photographs are by David Mager, Elbaliz Mendez, and Judy Mahoney
of the Pearson Learning Group Photo Studio except as noted below.
All photography © Pearson Education, Inc. (PEI) unless otherwise specifically noted.

Front Cover: *t.l.* © Scala/Art Resource, NY; *r.* The Art Archive/Egyptian Museum Cairo/Dagli Orti (A); *b.l.* © Melvyn P. Lawes/Papilio/Corbis.
Back Cover: © Werner Forman/Art Resource, NY. 1: The Art Archive/Dagli Orti. 4: © Giraudon/Art Resource, NY. 5: © Nigel Francis/Corbis.
6: Dagli Orti/The Art Archive. 7: *t.* © Erich Lessing/Art Resource, NY. 7: *b.* © Gianni Dagli Orti/Corbis. 8: *t.* The Art Archive/Musée du Louvre,
Paris/Dagli Orti. 8: *b.* © Ashmolean Museum/The Bridgeman Art Library. 9: © Erich Lessing/Art Resource, NY. 10: The Art Archive/Egyptian Museum
Cairo/Dagli Orti. 11: Lee Boltin/Boltin Picture Library. 12: *t.* © Werner Forman/Art Resource, NY. 12: *b.* © Erich Lessing/Art Resource, NY.
13: *t.* © Gianni Dagli Orti/Corbis. 13: *b.* The Art Archive/Musée du Louvre, Paris/Dagli Orti. 14: *l.* © Archivo Iconografico, S.A./Corbis.
14: *r.* The Art Archive/Museé du Louvre, Paris/Dagli Orti. 15: *t.* © Erich Lessing/Art Resource, NY. 15: *b.* The Art Archive/Musée du Louvre,
Paris/Dagli Orti. 16: © Scala/Art Resource, NY. 17: *l.* © Werner Forman/Art Resource, NY. 17: *r.* © 1983 The Metropolitan Museum of Art/
The Metropolitan Museum of Art Photograph Library. 18: © Vanni Archive/Corbis. 18–19: Karnak, Egypt/The Bridgeman Art Library.
19: © Scala/Art Resource, NY. 20: © Michael Nicholson/Corbis. 21: The Art Archive/Egyptian Museum Cairo/Dagli Orti. 22: © Wolfgang
Kaehler/Corbis. 23: *l.* © Erich Lessing/Art Resource, NY. 23: *m.* © Erich Lessing/Art Resource, NY. 23: *r.* © Erich Lessing/Art Resource, NY.
24: *t.* The Art Archive/Egyptian Museum Cairo/Dagli Orti. 24: *b.* Andreas Einsiedel/DK Images. 25: Dagli Orti/The Picture Desk/The Art
Archive/Kobal. 26: The Art Archive/Luxor Museum, Egypt/Dagli Orti. 27: The Art Archive/Dagli Orti. 28: The Art Archive/Dagli Orti.
29: *t.* © Werner Forman/Art Resource, NY. 29: *b.* The Art Archive/Dagli Orti
Illustration: 5: XNR Productions.

For information regarding licensing and permissions, write to Rights and Permissions Department, Pearson Learning Group,
299 Jefferson Road, Parsippany, NJ 07054 USA or to Rights and Permissions Department, DK Publishing,
The Penguin Group (UK), 80 Strand, London WC2R 0RL

Lexile is a U.S. registered trademark of MetaMetrics, Inc. All right reserved.

ISBN: 0-7652-5269-4

Color reproduction by Colourscan, Singapore
Printed in the United States of America
2 3 4 5 6 7 8 9 10   08 07 06 05

1-800-321-3106
www.pearsonlearning.com

Contents

Introduction

Hatshepsut (Hat-SHEP-soot) was a woman, yet she was a king of Egypt. How could this be? True, Hatshepsut had royal blood. She was the daughter, sister, wife, and aunt of Egyptian kings. Yet Hatshepsut wanted to be more than the relative of kings—she wanted to be king herself.

A few other women had ruled Egypt, usually holding the throne for a young son—but they did not claim the title of king. Hatshepsut became a female **pharaoh** (FARE-oh), the nation's most powerful leader.

How did Hatshepsut come to rule in a man's place, and how did she persuade Egyptians to accept and obey her? Her reign lasted more than twenty years and produced peace and wealth for Egypt, but she had powerful enemies. After her death, the record of her kingship was nearly destroyed. Who tried to erase this great ruler's legacy, and why?

statue of Hatshepsut holding vases with offerings to one of the Egyptian gods

The year of Hatshepsut's birth isn't certain, but records of related events show that she was born around 1500 B.C. This was during the period in Egypt's history known as the New Kingdom.

The New Kingdom, which lasted from approximately 1570 B.C. to 1070 B.C., was Egypt's golden age. Two countries, Lower and Upper Egypt, united under one ruler. Egypt **expanded** south into Nubia and east into what is now Syria. The capital city became Thebes, now called Luxor.

In the New Kingdom, the Great Pyramids of Giza were already more than 1,000 years old.

EGYPT

- Ancient site
- Modern city

Mediterranean Sea

Alexandria

Cairo
Giza
Memphis

LOWER EGYPT

Sinai Peninsula

N

MIDDLE EGYPT

Nile R.

| 0 | 100 | 200 mi |
| 0 | 100 | 200 km |

Deir el-Bahri

Karnak
Valley of the Kings
Thebes (modern Luxor)

Red Sea

present-day Egypt

UPPER EGYPT

AFRICA

Lake Nasser

N U B I A

Pharaoh's Daughter

In ancient Egypt, only half of all the children born survived and grew up. The other babies died, usually of disease. Death made no exception for royalty. Neferubity, Hatshepsut's sister, died in infancy. Hatshepsut—meaning "most **exalted** of ladies"—lived. Just by surviving birth, she earned the first of many royal titles to come: *sit nesu*, pharaoh's daughter.

Egyptian boys and girls shaved their heads except for one long lock on the side. Cutting off the sidelock was a symbol of passing from childhood to adulthood.

Egypt, Then and Now

	Ancient Egypt	Modern Egypt
Infant Mortality	30 to 50%	6%
Life Expectancy	30s	64
Literacy Rate	about 5%	51%
Major Religion	Polytheism (belief in many gods)	Islam
Capital	Thebes	Cairo
Language	Egyptian	Arabic
Government	Monarchy	Republic

This 70-foot **obelisk**, or four-sided pillar, was built during Thutmose I's reign.

All in the Thutmose Family

Hatshepsut's father was Thutmose I, a general. He had become pharaoh by marrying Ahmose, a royal. When they married, Ahmose's title changed from *senet nesu*, pharaoh's sister, to *hemet nesu weret*, pharaoh's great wife. There was no Egyptian word for *queen*.

Ahmose was a "great" wife because, like most pharaohs, Thutmose I would have more than one wife. Thutmose I and a lesser wife, Mutnofret, had four sons. Any one of them could have become pharaoh. However, the first three boys died young, before they had the opportunity to rule.

The boys' younger brother, Thutmose II, was the only surviving son of the pharaoh. Because Thutmose II had a different mother than Hatshepsut, he was her half-brother.

Statue of Thutmose I, Hatshepsut's father

A scribe is shown in this **relief**, a form of art with raised images, dating to about 2400 B.C.

Reading, Writing, and Royalty

The brother and sister both had an education, but in ancient Egypt, schooling was very different for boys than it was for girls. Thutmose II went to **scribe** school to learn reading and writing. He practiced military skills since, as pharaoh, he would be expected to lead troops into battle.

Girls weren't allowed to go to school. However, as a pharaoh's daughter, Hatshepsut received a royal education at the palace. Like her half-brother, she learned to read and write, but her main subject was the duty of a royal family member. Like her mother, she learned how to become a pharaoh's great wife. Ahmose, her mother, managed the palace and performed ceremonies. Raising the next pharaoh was an important part of a pharaoh's great wife's responsibilities.

Egyptian girls couldn't go to school. However, women worked, owned land, and filed lawsuits. Many ancient women had few of those rights. The woman shown here is grinding corn.

Pharaoh's Wife

Thutmose I outlived most Egyptians. He died in his fifties, an old man at a time when few people lived to be forty.

The death of the pharaoh was happy news for Egypt's enemies. A leaderless country could easily fall into a condition of chaos. Usually, there was no better time to attack.

Soon after Thutmose I's death, both Nubia to the south and Palestine to the east launched attacks against Egypt. They both quickly **retreated**, however, because Thutmose I had left behind a well-prepared army.

The pharaoh had also left a male heir. Thutmose II was clearly next in line to rule Egypt.

This relief from a pharaoh's temple shows warriors fighting.

the mummy of Thutmose II, the only surviving son of Thutmose I

Children in Charge

Thutmose II didn't have a drop of royal blood because both his father and his mother, Mutnofret, were common-born. So he did what every non-royal heir was expected to do: he married his royal half-sister, Hatshepsut, daughter of Ahmose. The marriage of sisters and brothers was common among ancient Egypt's royal families.

Though he became pharaoh, Thutmose II didn't lead Egypt's army in battle. He was either too young or possibly too sick to command the troops directly.

His bride, Hatshepsut, was probably older than Thutmose II. She was somewhere between the ages of twelve and fifteen when she became pharaoh's great wife.

Thutmose Family Tree

In the Thutmose family, royal blood passed down from female to female. Thutmose II and his only son, Thutmose III, both had common-born mothers who were secondary wives of the pharaoh. Thutmose III's wife, Meritre-Hatshepsut, was royal, but the identity of her parents is unclear.

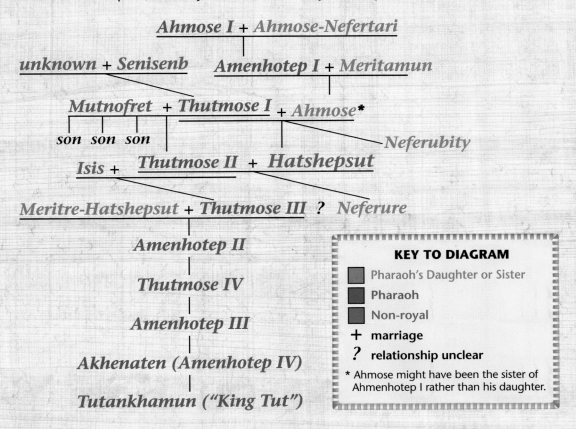

Ahmose I + *Ahmose-Nefertari*

unknown + *Senisenb*   *Amenhotep I* + *Meritamun*

Mutnofret + *Thutmose I* + *Ahmose**

son son son   *Neferubity*

Isis + *Thutmose II* + *Hatshepsut*

Meritre-Hatshepsut + *Thutmose III* **?** *Neferure*

Amenhotep II

Thutmose IV

Amenhotep III

Akhenaten (Amenhotep IV)

Tutankhamun ("King Tut")

KEY TO DIAGRAM

⬛ Pharaoh's Daughter or Sister

⬛ Pharaoh

⬛ Non-royal

+ marriage

? relationship unclear

* Ahmose might have been the sister of Ahmenhotep I rather than his daughter.

About Egyptian Names

When Egyptian mothers named their children, they often joined the name of an Egyptian god to a desirable trait. For example:

Merit (beloved) + **Re** (sun god) = **Meritre**

Nefer (beautiful) + **ka** (life spirit) + **Re** = **Neferkare**

Tut (image) + **ankh** (living) + **Amun** (hidden king of gods) = **Tutankhamun**

The pendant in this necklace is shaped like an eye, the symbol of protection and good health. A vulture goddess is on one side of the eye and a snake goddess is on the other.

What Did Hatshepsut Look Like?

Like most Egyptian women of her time, Hatshepsut was slender and petite, perhaps 5 feet tall or a little less. Her long nose was a typical Thutmose family trait.

She was probably bald, since many Egyptians—men, women, and children—shaved their heads to cool off in the hot desert. Hatshepsut wore wigs with long, coarse braids and curls. She outlined her eyes with kohl, a heavy, black powder. Her full-length dress, made of Egypt's finest linen, tied at the waist with a colorful sash.

For a ceremony, she might have put on large hoop earrings, up to a dozen rings, a wrist bracelet, an arm bracelet, an ankle bracelet, and a large neckpiece. Above all, perched regally on her head, sat the crown of pharaoh's great wife.

statue of Hatshepsut made from pink granite

statue of Isis, the mother of Thutmose III

This quotation comes from advice written during the Eighteenth Dynasty. It is part of a text known as *The Instruction of Any*.

Advice for Husbands

Do not control your wife in her house, when you know that she is efficient. Don't say to her: "Where is it? Get it!" when she has put it in the right place.

Amun, the secret king of gods

Amun's Wife

Hatshepsut's marriage echoed that of her mother, Ahmose. She and her husband had one surviving daughter, Neferure. Her husband and a secondary wife, Isis, had one surviving son, Thutmose III. Like Mutnofret, the mother of Thutmose II, Isis was a commoner, with no royal blood.

Unlike her mother, Hatshepsut held the title god's wife of Amun. Judging by her writings, it was her favorite title of all. It gave her an important role in the worship of the Egyptian god Amun. It was the highest position any woman could hold—but not for long.

Maatkare

Thutmose II died of an unknown cause at an unknown age when Hatshepsut was between fifteen and thirty years old. Her nephew and stepson, Thutmose III, a baby, was now pharaoh. Since he was too young to rule, Hatshepsut ruled for him as **regent**.

Hatshepsut's daughter, Neferure, and Thutmose III grew up at the palace together. One day, it was expected, the half-siblings would marry. First, though, the young pharaoh had to learn to walk and talk.

Thutmose III and Neferure

Re (Ra) was often shown with the head of a hawk.

The Rise to Power

Neferure's tutor, Senenmut, became Hatshepsut's closest advisor. He managed her lands and supervised the construction of monuments that showed her importance.

Over the next few years, Hatshepsut gradually changed from ruling in Thutmose III's place to being the sole ruler. An **inscription** made during this time referred to Hatshepsut as "one to whom Re [the sun god] has actually given the kingship." Hatshepsut was pharaoh in all but name.

A commoner named Senenmut raised and tutored little Neferure. He is seen holding Neferure in this statue.

As a female, however, Hatshepsut wasn't allowed to conduct certain ceremonies. She wasn't trained to lead an army. Her son, if she had one, would not inherit the throne. Finally, she would have to give up her power as soon as Thutmose III came of age.

Some Egyptian Gods

Amun (or Amen) was the secret king of gods. Several pharaohs carried his name: Amenhotep I, II, and III, and Tutankhamun ("King Tut").

Re (or Ra), the sun god, was most revered in northern Egypt. Amun dominated the south. During the New Kingdom, people worshiped these gods together as **Amun-Re** or **Amun-Ra**.

Thoth was the god of the moon, magic, and writing. Thutmose I, II, III, and IV were named for him.

Thoth was often shown with the head of an ibis, a bird.

A Woman King

By her seventh year as regent, Hatshepsut did the unthinkable. She boldly declared herself a female pharaoh, a title that didn't exist. She held a **coronation** ceremony in which she was crowned. Some scholars think her reign as pharaoh began around 1473 B.C., although others believe she started to rule at an earlier date.

For her pharaoh name, she selected Maatkare, which means "Maat is the life spirit of Re." Now, no one, not even Thutmose III, outranked her. She was the most powerful person in all of Egypt, for as long as she lived.

There was a problem: Would the people believe her bold claim? Would they obey her commands?

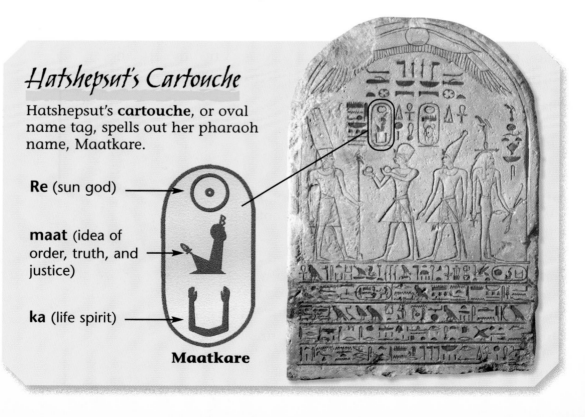

Hatshepsut's Cartouche

Hatshepsut's **cartouche**, or oval name tag, spells out her pharaoh name, Maatkare.

Re (sun god)

maat (idea of order, truth, and justice)

ka (life spirit)

Maatkare

This obelisk shows Hatshepsut, who is dressed as a pharaoh, being crowned by the god Amun.

To the Egyptians, a woman could not be pharaoh in place of a man. However, those who opposed Hatshepsut's move were afraid to protest.

Hatshepsut had too much power. She had risen slowly, in small steps, while gathering support. Many of her advisors had served under her father, Thutmose I, and her husband, Thutmose II. She had also appointed her own loyal staff, including Senenmut.

Her advisors had good reason to support her. The more power that she had, the more power came to them. Senenmut, for instance, held many important titles while he served Hatshepsut. One was overseer of the works of the king.

Like other pharaohs, Hatshepsut wore a long, false beard. It linked pharaohs to Egyptian gods, who also wore beards.

Hatshepsut had four tall obelisks built. Writings on all sides boasted of her greatness and that of her father.

Power and Glory

Hatshepsut began to appear in men's clothing with the royal symbols of a male pharaoh. She wore a knee-length kilt, a pharaoh's shoulder-length headdress, and a false beard.

As Thutmose III grew, he surely came to understand what his aunt had done. He was the true pharaoh, yet he never challenged Hatshepsut. Instead, he continued his education and military training and let "Maatkare" rule.

Why did Hatshepsut declare she was a pharaoh? Was she a power-hungry woman who took advantage of her nephew's youth, or was there a more practical reason for her to become pharaoh?

Duties of a Pharaoh

* establish and collect taxes
* store food in case of drought
* initiate and oversee construction
* initiate trade with other countries
* protect Egypt from enemies
* lead troops into battle
* represent the people to their gods, and the gods to the people
* preserve *maat*, the concept of order, truth, and justice

Hatshepsut believed her kingship was *maat*, true and just. Her pharaoh name, Maatkare, said so. Maat was the Egyptian goddess of order, truth, and justice. Egyptians believed Maat helped to judge the dead. A dead person's heart was weighed on a scale against the feather of Maat. If the person had lived a good life, the heart and feather balanced.

It is true that Thutmose III was too young to lead the army. Hatshepsut might have seized power in order to protect Egypt against enemies that might want to invade. If so, her bold move made Egypt look bold, too, and perhaps it helped maintain order at a time of chaos. However, she still needed to make her people believe that her claim to the throne was valid.

feather

Hatshepsut making an offering to the god Amun.

the goddess Maat

Temples and Tombs

All the pharaohs before Hatshepsut wrote their life stories on the walls of temples and tombs. Hatshepsut had more reason to boast and even lie about her greatness than any pharaoh. Her claim to the throne was unique and questionable. She made up a long birth story to "prove" she was a genuine pharaoh.

Hatshepsut built one of ancient Egypt's greatest temples at a place called Deir al-Bahri. She had the birth story carved on the temple walls. It said that the god Amun was her father and that he had named her pharaoh. Then, the story continued, her real father, Thutmose I, had also named her pharaoh before he died. That was a lie, since Thutmose I had named Thutmose II as the next pharaoh.

Hatshepsut's temple still stands in modern-day Luxor, Egypt.

red granite sphinx of Hatshepsut

Walls That Tell Stories

Though built during her lifetime, Hatshepsut's beautiful temple, designed by Senenmut, was meant to honor her after her death. The building had three levels, connected by ramps, that rose into the surrounding cliffs.

Inside the temple were shrines dedicated to Hatshepsut's special gods, including Amun. As Hatshepsut's reign went on, she added carvings that celebrated her accomplishments. There were many statues of Hatshepsut. Some showed her as a **sphinx** with a pharaoh's head and a lion's body.

Fewer than 5 percent of Egyptians could read hieroglyphics.

Hatshepsut's audience for her stories was not the Egyptian people. Few Egyptians could read **hieroglyphics**, writing in which pictures stand for either words or sounds. Even if they could, they weren't allowed in temples. Only royals, priests, and scribes saw the writings.

Those were all important people, and Hatshepsut needed them on her side. Yet they weren't as important to her as people who were not yet born. One of Hatshepsut's obelisks explained her deep desire to tell her life story to future generations.

Now my heart turns to and fro,
In thinking what will the people say,
They who shall see my monument in after years,
And shall speak of what I have done.

Trade, Not War

In the ninth year of her reign, Hatshepsut truly had something to boast about. As pharaoh, she was expected to lead the Egyptian army into war, but she did not need to do that. While her armies defended Egypt's lands, Hatshepsut was not a conqueror. Instead, she led Egypt into trade.

Her desert nation needed trees for building ships. Hatshepsut's traders bought lots of wood in Phoenicia to the north. From Sinai to the east, they brought back copper, turquoise, and other minerals.

Hatshepsut's greatest trade mission was to the land of Punt, far to the south. We don't know exactly where Punt was located. It might have been in present-day Ethiopia or Somalia. No Egyptian had traveled there in centuries.

These reliefs from Hatshepsut's temple show scenes from the voyage to Punt.

sailors in the rigging of a ship

a village with palm trees, birds, and thatched huts

unloading goods from a ship

Hatshepsut sent five boats filled with trade goods, with thirty rowers per boat, over the Red Sea to Punt. Her Egyptian traders learned that Puntites lived in domed houses built on stilts. The queen of Punt was very large, a wonderment to the slender Egyptians. Leopards, giraffes, monkeys, baboons, and other strange animals lived in this African land.

The traders returned with boatloads of luxuries and rare goods. Hatshepsut had the details of the trip carved on the walls of her temple. She wrote that Amun himself had told her to go to Punt and had made the journey a success.

The text also said that Hatshepsut was the first pharaoh ever to reach the land of Punt, which wasn't true. She was using the voyage to further polish her image as a pharaoh.

The Egyptians were amazed by the appearance of the queen of Punt.

Trading Places

These trade items provide clues to Punt's climate and culture, though its exact location is not known.

Egypt Traded . . .	. . . for These Items From Punt
beads, necklaces, cowrie shells (a form of currency), bread, beverages, meat, fruits, axes, and daggers	ebony wood, ivory tusks, **myrrh** trees, animal skins (leopard, for example), live baboons and monkeys, a giraffe, short-horned cattle, silver, and gold

Erased From History

Hatshepsut's reign lasted for about twenty years. During that time, she defended Egypt's borders and fed her people. She brought in luxuries and other goods through trade and built some of Egypt's greatest structures. She raised Thutmose III, now an outstanding warrior in his twenties. She had preserved *maat*, the idea of justice, truth, and order.

Then, Hatshepsut died, somewhere in her late thirties to early fifties. Her death might have taken place in 1458 B.C. Thutmose III gave his aunt and stepmother a burial fit for a pharaoh. Without question, he honored her and her unique title. Then he took his place as sole pharaoh.

Soon after, Syria and Palestine attacked Egypt. Thutmose III led his army in defeating them. He didn't stop there. In seventeen battles over many years, he took Kadesh, Megiddo, and other cities, expanding Egypt's borders.

Hatshepsut's mummy has never been found. A jar similar to the ones shown here held her preserved liver.

Thutmose III

The Glorious Reign of Thutmose III

These victories brought peace. No one dared attack the mighty Egyptian army. Now, Thutmose III's goal was to make sure his son, Amenhotep II, would rule after him.

Though it is logical that Thutmose III would have married Neferure, scholars aren't sure. In any event, Neferure died. The mother of Amenhotep II was a lesser royal.

By the time Thutmose III was in his early fifties, he had ruled for twenty-five glorious years. His place in history as a great Egyptian pharaoh was secure.

That is when the destruction began. Under Thutmose III's rule, Egyptians attempted to erase every trace of Maatkare, their female pharaoh.

Destroying the Woman King

Workers smashed to tiny pieces some 200 of the woman king's sphinxes and statues. They gouged out the eyes and cut off the noses of other statues and even tried to burn the stone. They hacked off writings and images from stone walls, including those at her temple. They left some stories in place but put Thutmose III's name in place of Hatshepsut's.

Records of Hatshepsut, the pharaoh's great wife and pharaoh's daughter, were untouched. Only Maatkare, the female pharaoh, was erased and spoiled. Thutmose III had accepted his aunt's reign for many years. What had changed—why did he try to erase her memory?

This carving was intentionally damaged during Thutmose III's reign to erase the center image of Hatshepsut.

Maatkare Mystery

It is possible that Thutmose III acted out of anger and revenge. After all, Hatshepsut stole her nephew's title and kept it for about twenty years. Yet, if anger was his reason, why did Thutmose III wait so long to express it? As soon as he became pharaoh, he was the most powerful man in the land. His people had to carry out all of his orders.

It is possible that Thutmose III acted to protect his son,

Amenhotep II. The young heir had not yet begun his rule as pharaoh. Hatshepsut was not his mother, and he didn't carry her royal blood in his veins. Erasing Maatkare left a direct line of males: Thutmose I, Thutmose II, Thutmose III, and Amenhotep II. Thutmose III dated his reign from the death of his father, Thutmose II—not the death of Hatshepsut.

Amenhotep II

Maatkare may have become pharaoh to preserve *maat*. It is possible that preserving *maat* was also a reason to destroy her memory. Her supporters were dead, and surely there were many Egyptians who had not approved of the woman king. Rather than defend a very unusual reign, perhaps the Thutmose family found it easier to simply erase it.

The Maatkare mystery is unsolved. A few dozen statues and writings escaped destruction. Today, 3,500 years later, these provide all that we know about the woman pharaoh of Egypt.

Maatkare, the woman king

Archaeologists worked for years to restore Hatshepsut's Red Chapel. The building had once housed the barge of Amun-Re, a boat that held an image of the god. Over half of the original blocks were used to recreate the chapel, which opened to the public in 2001.

Possible Timeline of Events

Each time a pharaoh came to power, Egyptians began a new calendar. The first year of the reign was Year 1, the second year was Year 2, and so on. Experts can't always match Egyptian dates to modern dates. This timeline starts about 1525 B.C. to 1504 B.C. and ends about 1450 B.C. to 1427 B.C.

1525 B.C. to 1504 B.C. — Thutmose I

▶ Year 1
Sometime between 1525 B.C.–1504 B.C., Thutmose I, a general, marries Ahmose, a royal, and becomes pharaoh.

▶ Year 2–5
Somewhere around 1500 B.C., Hatshepsut is born.

▶ Year 10–15
Thutmose I dies in his fifties.

Thutmose II

▶ Year 1
Hatshepsut marries her half-brother, Thutmose II, the new pharaoh.

▶ Year 2–7
Hatshepsut and Thutmose II's daughter, Neferure, is born. Thutmose II has a son, Thutmose III, by another wife.

▶ Year 3–15
Thutmose II dies.

Thutmose III/Hatshepsut — 1450 B.C. to 1427 B.C.

▼ Year 1
Hatshepsut is the regent for Thutmose III, an infant.

▼ Year 5
Hatshepsut adopts a pharaoh's name: Maatkare.

▼ Year 9
Hatshepsut sponsors a trading voyage to the land of Punt.

▼ Year 22
Hatshepsut dies and has a pharaoh's burial, around 1458 B.C. Thutmose III leads the first of seventeen war campaigns.

▼ Year 46–51
Images and writings of Hatshepsut as pharaoh are destroyed.

▼ Year 2–4
Hatshepsut appears in carvings as regent, but Senenmut calls her "one to whom Re has actually given the kingship."

▼ Year 7
She declares herself pharaoh and dresses as a male, possibly around 1473 B.C.

▼ Year 15–16
Four obelisks honor Hatshepsut; her father, Thutmose I; and the god Amun.

▼ Year 33
Thutmose III's victories establish a period of peace, power, and wealth.

▼ Year 53
Thutmose III dies. Amenhotep II, his son, is pharaoh.

Glossary

cartouche — the oval name tag of a pharaoh

coronation — the act of crowning a ruler

exalted — raised to a high position; glorified

expanded — increased in size

hieroglyphics — writing in which pictures stand for words or sounds

inscription — writing carved in stone

myrrh — a tree resin (sap) used to create incense

obelisk — a tall, thin, pointed monument with four sides

pharaoh — a ruler of ancient Egypt

regent — one who rules in the place or absence of another

relief — a form of artwork with raised surfaces

retreated — withdrew from a position in battle

scribe — a scholar who recorded events such as war victories

sphinx — an ancient Egyptian image in the form of a lion with the head of a human or animal

Index